EARLY PEOPLES

AFRICANS OF THE GHANA, MALI, AND SONGHAI EMPIRES

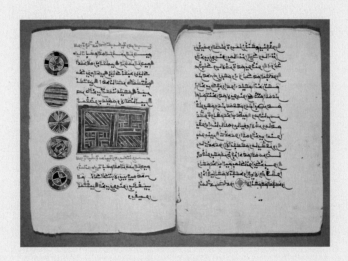

WORLD BOOK

World Book
a Scott Fetzer company
Chicago
www.worldbookonline.com

World Book, Inc.
233 N. Michigan Avenue
Chicago, IL 60601
U.S.A.

For information about other World Book publications, visit our Web site at
http://www.worldbookonline.com or call 1-800-WORLDBK (967-5325).
For information about sales to schools and libraries, call 1-800-975-3250
(United States), or 1-800-837-5365 (Canada).

Library of Congress Cataloging-in-Publication Data

Africans of the Ghana, Mali, and Songhai empires.
    p. cm. -- (Early peoples)
    Includes index.
    Summary: "A discussion of the Ghana, Mali, and Songhai
people of Africa, including who they were, where they lived,
the rise of civilization, social structure, religion, art
and architecture, science and technology, daily life,
entertainment and sports, and fall of civilization. Features
include timelines, fact boxes, glossary, list of recommended
reading and web sites, and index"--Provided by publisher.
    ISBN 978-0-7166-2134-8
    1. Mali (Empire)--Juvenile literature. 2. Ghana (Empire)--
Juvenile literature. 3. Songhai Empire--Juvenile literature.
4. Africa, West--History--To 1884--Juvenile literature.
I. World Book, Inc.
DT532.15.A38 2009
966'.02--dc22
                                        2008021467

Printed in China
1 2 3 4 5 13 12 11 10 09

STAFF

EXECUTIVE COMMITTEE
President
  Paul A. Gazzolo
Vice President and Chief Marketing Officer
  Patricia Ginnis
Vice President and Chief Financial Officer
  Donald D. Keller
Vice President and Editor in Chief
  Paul A. Kobasa
Director, Human Resources
  Bev Ecker
Chief Technology Officer
  Tim Hardy
Managing Director, International
  Benjamin Hinton

EDITORIAL
Editor in Chief
  Paul A. Kobasa
Associate Director, Supplementary Publications
  Scott Thomas
Managing Editor, Supplementary Publications
  Barbara A. Mayes
Senior Editor, Supplementary Publications
  Kristina Vaicikonis
Manager, Research, Supplementary Publications
  Cheryl Graham
Manager, Contracts & Compliance
(Rights & Permissions)
  Loranne K. Shields
Administrative Assistant
  Ethel Matthews

Editors
  Nicholas Kilzer
  Scott Richardson
  Christine Sullivan

GRAPHICS AND DESIGN
Associate Director
  Sandra M. Dyrlund
Manager
  Tom Evans
Coordinator, Design Development and
Production
  Brenda B. Tropinski

EDITORIAL ADMINISTRATION
Director, Systems and Projects
  Tony Tills
Senior Manager, Publishing Operations
  Timothy Falk

PRODUCTION
Director, Manufacturing and Pre-Press
  Carma Fazio
Manufacturing Manager
  Steve Hueppchen
Production/Technology Manager
  Anne Fritzinger
Production Specialist
  Curley Hunter
Proofreader
  Emilie Schrage

MARKETING
Chief Marketing Officer
  Patricia Ginnis
Associate Director, School and Library
Marketing
  Jennifer Parello

Produced for World Book by
  White-Thomson Publishing Ltd,
  +44 (0)845 362 8240
  www.wtpub.co.uk
  Steve White-Thomson, President

Writer: Lisa Klobuchar
Editor: Kelly Davis
Designer: Simon Borrough
Photo Researcher: Amy Sparks
Map Artist: Stefan Chabluk
Illustrator: Adam Hook (p. 15)
Fact Checker: Charlene Rimsa
Proofreader: Catherine Gardner
Indexer: Nila Glikin

Consultant:
Timothy Insoll
Professor of Archaeology
University of Manchester
Manchester, United Kingdom

TABLE OF CONTENTS

Glossary There is a glossary on pages 60-61. Terms defined in the glossary are in type **that looks like this** on their first appearance on any spread (two facing pages).

Additional Resources Books for further reading and recommended Web sites are listed on page 62. Because of the nature of the Internet, some Web site addresses may have changed since publication. The publisher has no responsibility for any such changes or for the content of cited sources.

WHO WERE THE PEOPLE OF GHANA, MALI, AND SONGHAI?

The people of Ghana *(GAH nuh)*, Mali *(MAH lee)*, and Songhai *(sawng GY* or *SAWNG hy)* lived in the thriving commercial empires of **medieval** West Africa.

The empire of Ghana was probably founded during the A.D. 300's. This empire reached its height in about A.D. 1000, when it included parts of what are now the countries of Mali and Mauritania *(MAWR ih TAY nee uh)*. During the 1200's, Mali replaced Ghana as West Africa's most powerful empire. The Mali Empire included parts of what are now the countries of Burkina-Faso *(bur KEE nuh FAH soh)*, Gambia, Guinea *(GIHN ee)*, the modern country of Mali, Mauritania, Niger, and Senegal *(SEHN uh GAWL)*. By 1500, most of the Mali Empire had come under the control of the Songhai Empire. The Songhai Empire covered about the same geographic area as the empire of Mali. The Songhai Empire ended in the 1590's.

The Land

The empires of Ghana, Mali, and Songhai were located in a large region of West Africa called the **Sahel** *(sah HEHL)*. The Sahel is a dry grassland south of the Sahara Desert. The Sahel was also called the

▼ The Great Mosque of Djenne *(jeh NAY)*, in Mali. **Mosques** have occupied this site since the 1200's, during the rule of the Mali Empire. The Great Mosque was built from mud bricks, or **adobe,** in the early 1900's. Buildings of adobe were common in the medieval West African empires.

▲ At the heart of the medieval West African empires was the dry grassland region called the Sahel. Small villages can still be seen on the plains of the Sahel today.

Sudan *(soo DAN)*. The three great West African kingdoms were located in what was known as western Sudan. The Niger River flows through the heart of this region. The river was an important source of water and food for the peoples of West Africa, and they also used the Niger for transportation.

Empires Built on Trade

The West African empires were made up of a number of smaller kingdoms united under a central government. The rulers of these empires expanded their lands by conquering surrounding kingdoms. They gained power and wealth through their control of trade between northern Africa and the region south of the Sahel. Traders brought gold from the south. They exchanged gold for salt and copper from Saharan mines, dried fruits from northern Africa, woven cloth from Europe, and finely crafted objects from the Middle East. Such cities as Gao *(gah OH)* and Timbuktu *(tihm BUHK too)* became busy commercial centers.

SUDAN AND SAHEL

The name *Sudan* comes from the Arabic *Bilal as-Sudan (bih LAHL so DAN)*, which means "southern country." This area is not related to the modern-day country of Sudan, which lies farther east.

The name *Sahel* comes from the Arabic word for "shore." To Arabic travelers, the Sahara seemed like a vast sea of sand. Reaching the grasslands of the Sahel was always a great relief, which they compared to arriving on land after a long voyage.

THE GHANA EMPIRE

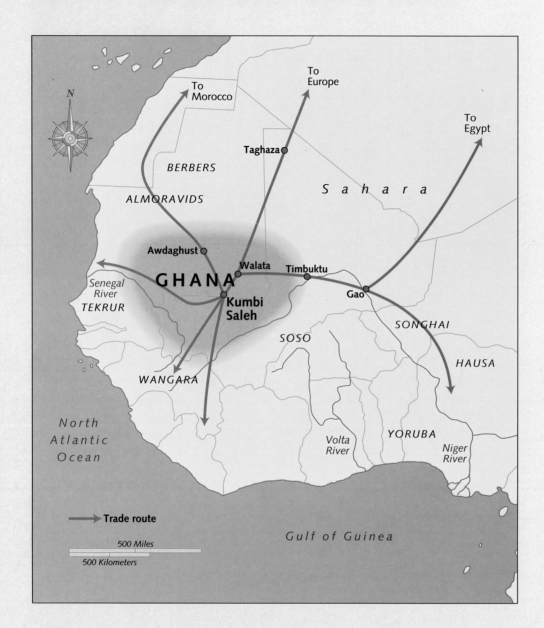

◄ The Ghana Empire as it existed in about A.D. 1050 is shown in pink. Trade routes, shown in red, stretched from Ghana's capital city, Kumbi Saleh, across western Africa and beyond.

The first great empire to appear on the plains of West Africa was called the Ghana Empire. No one is sure exactly when this empire arose. Evidence suggests that an African people called the Soninke *(soh NIHNG kay)* started the first Ghana kingdom as early as the A.D. 200's. They called their empire Wagadu *(WAHG uh DOO)*. Outsiders used the name Ghana for the empire. Ghana meant "war chief" and was the title used for the Soninke kings.

A Growing Empire

The Soninke founded a capital city, Kumbi Saleh *(KOOM be sah LAY)*, in what is now southwestern Mauritania. Productive farming, rich supplies of gold, and control of the Sahara Desert **trade routes** made the people of Kumbi Saleh wealthy and powerful. The Sahara trade routes linked west-central Africa with the Mediterranean Sea. Taxes on goods entering and leaving the empire made the rulers very rich.

Ghana began to grow into an empire in the 900's. It did so by defeating neighboring kingdoms and by conquering a key trading city in the Sahara called Awdaghust *(ah dah GOHST)*. Close trade relationships developed between the **Muslims** of northern Africa and the people of Ghana, who practiced traditional African religions. Muslims were successful traders and merchants in the empire. Many Muslims held positions of power in the Ghana Empire.

Decline

The empire reached its height in about 1050; then, it slowly began to lose power, partly because of conflicts with powerful Muslims. By 1100, Kumbi Saleh was controlled by a **Berber** people from the north, the **Almoravids** *(AL muh RAHV uhdz)*. Some historians believe that the Almoravids took control by conquering the city in 1076. But the Almoravid takeover may have happened peacefully.

The empire of Ghana broke up into a number of separate kingdoms. One of these kingdoms was Soso *(soo soo)*. In about 1203, the Sosos conquered Ghana's capital, along with several other small Ghanaian states. The Sosos joined these states into one larger kingdom.

How Do We Know?

Much of the information on the Ghana Empire has been passed down through storytelling and through the writings of the Spanish-**Arab** scholar and geographer Al-Bakri *(ahl BAHK ree)*. Al-Bakri was born in the 1000's. In 1068, he wrote *Book of the Routes and Realms*, an account of Muslim Spain and northern Africa. Studies by **archaeologists** *(AHR kee OL uh jihstz)* have supported many of the descriptions in the writings of Al-Bakri.

▼ A doorway, decorated in Arabic style, in an **adobe** building in Walata *(wah lah TAH)*. This city was an important stop on the Saharan trade routes in the Ghana Empire.

THE MALI EMPIRE

The peoples living under Soso rule in the early 1200's included the Malinke *(muh LIHNG kee* or *muh LIHNG kay)*. Their kingdom was in present-day Guinea, and it was ruled by a **clan**, or group of related families, called the Keitas *(KAY tahz)*. Under ruler Sundiata Keita *(sun JAHT ah KAY tah)*, the Malinke overthrew the Soso in about 1240 and founded the Mali Empire. Over the next few decades, the Mali rulers brought the kingdoms surrounding their region under a strong central government.

A Large and Powerful Empire

The Mali Empire stretched from the coastal areas on the Atlantic Ocean west for about 1,500 miles (2,400 kilometers). Like Ghana, Mali's wealth was based mainly on its rich gold mines and the government's control over the **trade routes** that crossed the Sahara. Mansa Musa *(MAHN sah MOO sah)*, who reigned from 1312 to about 1337, made Mali the political and cultural power of West Africa. The empire's strong central government and powerful army made life safe

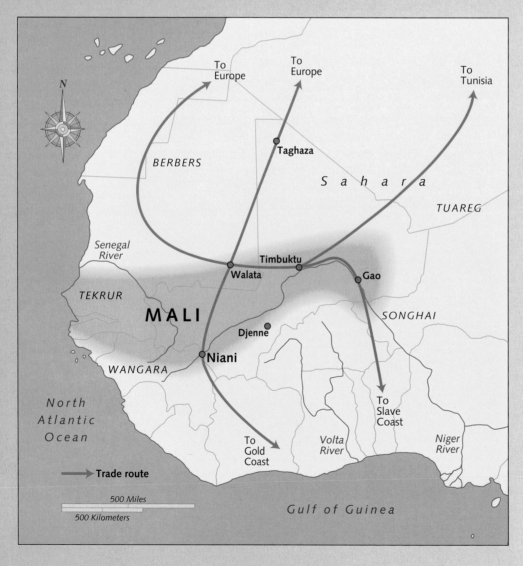

◀ The Mali Empire as it existed in about A.D. 1337 is shown in pink. Trade routes, shown in red, stretched from Niani *(nih AH nee)*, across western Africa toward Europe, Tunisia, and the coast of the Gulf of Guinea.

and secure, and merchants and traders carried on their business without fear.

How Did the Mali People Live?

The kingdoms of the Mali Empire were part of several linked African cultures, which included the Bambara *(bahm BAH rah)*, Soninke, and Mandinka *(man DIHNG kay)*, sometimes called the Mandingo *(man DIHNG goh)*. Most of the cultures, in turn, were part of a larger cultural group called the Mande *(MAHN day)*. The Mande spoke related languages and carried on similar traditional ways of life. Most Mande societies were divided into **castes.** Farmers were the top **social class** for commoners. **Artisans,** such as blacksmiths and leatherworkers, were below the farmers in status, and slaves had the lowest status of all. The kings of the Mali Empire were **Muslims,** who blended traditional Mande religious and social customs with **Islam.**

MANSA MUSA

Mansa Musa greatly expanded the empire of Mali. He brought the trading cities of Gao and Timbuktu under his rule and made Timbuktu a center of learning. Mansa Musa spread Islam throughout the empire. In 1324, he traveled to Mecca *(MEHK uh)*, the holy city of the Muslims. Mansa Musa traveled in a **caravan** with thousands of companions. His senior wife traveled with him and brought along 500 serving women and slaves. Camels were loaded with gold and other gifts. When Mansa Musa arrived in Cairo, he spent and gave away so much gold that the value of the precious metal went down and stayed down for many years afterward. When he returned from his **pilgrimage,** Mansa Musa brought back many learned people, including an architect who designed **mosques** for Gao and Timbuktu.

▼ A shrine, built in the A.D. 200's in the present-day city of Kangaba *(can GAH BAH)*, is dedicated to the Keita clan. The ancestor of the Keitas was the legendary Sundiata, founder of the Mali Empire.

THE SONGHAI EMPIRE

The people known as Songhai became a political power during the A.D. 700's. In about 1010, the ruling Songhai king converted to **Islam**. That king set up a capital at Gao, a city on the Niger River in what is now the country of Mali. Mansa Musa made Gao part of the Mali Empire in 1325. Gao became independent in about 1375. Songhai arose as an empire after the decline of the Mali Empire. By the 1400's, Songhai had more power and wealth than any other empire in West Africa.

Songhai Emperors

Two emperors, Sunni Ali *(SUN ee AHL ee)* and Askia Muhammad *(AS kee ah moo HAM uhd)*, strengthened the empire more than any other rulers. Sunni Ali, a great warrior, reigned from about 1464 to 1492. He conquered many kingdoms and drove **Muslim** peoples, including the **Tuareg** *(TWAH rehg)*, out of Songhai lands. Sunni Ali captured the city of Djenne after a seven-year **siege** *(seej)*. He began a unified system of law and order, central government, and trade.

◀ The Songhai Empire as it existed in about A.D. 1500 is shown in pink. **Trade routes,** shown in red, linked Songhai's major cities and extended beyond toward Europe, Tunisia, and the coast of the Gulf of Guinea.

▲ A modern-day settlement on an island on the Niger River looks similar to those built centuries ago. The founders of the Songhai Empire lived along the Niger.

Askia Muhammad—also known as Askia I, or Askia the Great—became king in 1493. Songhai reached its peak under his rule. Askia I reorganized the government, expanded trade, and encouraged the practice of Islam. Askia's son forced him from the throne in 1528.

Songhai Government

Under Sunni Ali, the empire was divided into five **provinces.** He named a governor to head each province. Each governor in turn had staff working for him. Askia Muhammad improved on this system. He followed the Islamic belief in equality—that all people deserved the same chance to succeed. So, he gave government posts to people according to their education and ability, not according to the class level of their family. Among the five governors, one had more power than the other four. Every town had an appointed mayor, all of whom were Muslims.

ROYAL TITLES

The traditional title for kings among the Songhai people was *dia*. In about 1335, the Songhai kings began to use the title *sunni*. The last emperor to be called *sunni* was Sunni Baru, who ruled from 1492 to 1493. Muhammad Turay was the first to use the title *askia*, which was a high rank in the Songhai military. After Askia Muhammad, nine other Songhai rulers took the title *askia*.

GOLD, SALT, COPPER, AND IRON

The empires of Ghana, Mali, and Songhai gained their wealth largely from the trade in gold and salt. By the late 700's, the gold trade was so widespread in West Africa that the **Arab** geographer al-Fazari *(AHL faz AHR ee)* called Ghana "the land of gold."

Throughout the Ghana, Mali, and Songhai periods, miners removed huge amounts of gold from gold fields in what is now Senegal. The gold miners kept the exact location of the mines a closely guarded secret from foreigners. Modern **archaeologists** believe that from ancient times through the 1500's, West African miners produced about 10 tons (9 metric tons) of gold every year.

Gold for Salt

Although the West African empires were rich in gold, they were poor in salt. Huge salt deposits, however, lay beneath the Sahara Desert. The largest salt mines were in what is now the northern region of the country of Mali. These mines were in operation as early as A.D. 500.

THE VALUE OF SALT

Why was salt so valuable? Salt is an important part of people's diet. In the hot, dry climate of western Africa, sweat flushes much of the salt from a person's body. That salt must be replaced. In the past, before refrigeration, salt was also used in preserving food. Salt was not naturally present in the inland regions of the West African empires. So the people of this region traded a precious substance they had in abundance—gold—for a precious substance they lacked.

▼ Slabs of salt are stacked for trade in present-day Mali. Salt was as precious as gold throughout **medieval** West Africa.

Muslim merchants led camels loaded with salt southwest across the desert. One camel could carry a slab of salt weighing around 350 pounds (160 kilograms). Merchants traded salt for equal amounts of gold in the many trading centers of the West African empires.

Copper

Africans valued copper, with its reddish shine, for making beads and jewelry. In addition, after A.D. 1000, Africans used copper as money. In the 1300's, copper mines operated outside the borders of the Mali Empire. In the south, merchants traded copper for equal weights of gold, as well as salt and other valuable goods.

Iron

Iron was the base upon which the wealth of the West African empires was founded. It was a knowledge of iron-working that drove the region's flourishing trade and commerce. Iron tools allowed for efficient farming and for effective weapons for hunting. Iron-working was so important that it took on spiritual significance in the empires of West Africa. Items forged of iron also were used in West Africa as a form of money.

▲ A neck ring made out of copper mixed with other metals. West Africans prized copper for making jewelry.

TRADE

Gold was a valuable natural resource for the Ghana, Mali, and Songhai empires. But what made the empires truly wealthy and powerful was control of the **trade routes**. Taxing the goods that entered and left the empires created much of their fabulous wealth.

Long Distance Trade

Trade routes crisscrossed the empires, connecting the region of western **Sudan** with cities throughout northern Africa, such as Fez *(fehz)*, Marrakech *(MAR uh KEHSH)*, Tripoli *(TRIHP uh lee)*, and Cairo *(KY roh)*. From the north, merchants brought Asian silks; horses; cowrie *(KOW ree)* shells from the Indian Ocean, which were used as money; books written in Arabic; swords, knives, and kitchen utensils from Europe and the Middle East; and especially salt. At their lively marketplaces, West Africans eagerly received these foreign goods in exchange for cattle, cotton cloth, dried and salted fish, hides, ivory, wood, and especially gold. Slaves were also bought and sold in the cities of western Africa.

▼ Goods are traded from boats on the Niger River in present-day Mali.

PROTECTING TRADE

The government and laws of the West African empires were set up to protect the trade that created the wealth. In all three of the empires, the ruler oversaw a strong central government.

By the time of the Songhai Empire, the government's **civil service** was large and well organized. Both military and civilian, or nonmilitary, leaders helped the emperor run the central government. The civil service of Songhai helped to keep the empire running at its best, making certain that no disruption unsettled the vital trade on which the empire depended.

▲ A market in the Mali Empire in the 1400's is imagined in this depiction.

Local Trade

Traders carried food products throughout the kingdoms. In the Mali Empire, rice grown in the east was transported inland and traded for iron. Grain merchants sold millet *(MIHL iht)* and sorghum *(SAWR guhm)* in cities such as Timbuktu and at the salt mines of Taghaza *(tah GAH zah)*. Local trade in food also thrived in the West African empires. In the empire of Mali, farmers, fishermen, and herders traded their products with one another. In Songhai, **nomadic** fishermen sailed up and down the Niger River, selling fish in the towns.

Even though trade was important, only a small percentage of the people made their living as merchants. These people were mostly **Muslims** of **Arab** or West African descent. They generally lived apart from the rest of the population. In the Mali Empire, Muslim merchants had high status.

CARAVANS ACROSS THE SANDS

Merchants and traders traveled throughout West Africa in large groups called **caravans**. The traders used camels to carry their goods. The average caravan included about 1,000 camels. The **Arab** historian Ibn Khaldun (*IHB uhn khahl DOON*) reported caravans made up of 12,000 camels in the 1300's, however, so caravans could be much larger.

A Long Road

To travel between two cities in the Mali Empire—from Sijilmasa (*sih jihl MAHS uh*) on the northern edge of the Sahara Desert to Walata

▲ Camel caravans remain a vital means of transporting goods across the Sahara Desert, as they did at the height of the Mali Empire.

THE LOST CARAVAN

Crossing the desert was very hard. Caravans were sometimes attacked by robbers. Sometimes caravans were lost in sand-storms. In 1960, a French **archaeologist** found the remains of a caravan that had been lost in the desert in the 1100's. The cargo included some 2,000 copper rods.

on the southern edge—took two months. Because there were no roads in the desert, experienced guides had to lead the caravans. Caravans set out at sunrise and walked until the midday sun made it too hot to continue. Then they rested until afternoon and continued until nighttime. Wells provided water along the route, but they were often spaced far apart. Camels carried containers of water. But when water ran out, travelers would sometimes have to kill a camel and drink the water from the animal's stomach.

"Ships of the Desert"

Camels have a number of features and abilities that make them ideal for carrying heavy loads across the vast Saharan "sea of sand." They can travel great distances with little food or water. A camel has a built-in food supply on its back. Its hump is a large lump of fat that provides energy if food becomes scarce. A camel's wide feet make walking on soft sand easy. They can carry loads of up to 330 pounds (150 kilograms) for eight hours. For these reasons, they were often called "ships of the desert."

In a caravan, camels usually were attached in groups of 40. Each camel was linked to the saddle of the camel in front of it by a rope attached to a nose ring. Three or four camels walked side by side.

▼ Caravans crossing the vast Sahara Desert were sometimes lost and even buried by sand storms.

MAJOR CITIES

The major cities of the western **Sudan** region were centers of trade, culture, and learning. Peoples of many different backgrounds lived there, and a number of languages could be heard in the streets and marketplaces.

Kumbi Saleh

Archaeological digs in the early to mid-1900's and in the 1980's uncovered the remains of Kumbi Saleh, the capital of the Ghana Empire. **Archaeologists** found evidence of a densely populated town with narrow streets and closely packed houses. The town was made up of two main sections. The area where the Islamic merchants lived was on the northeast. Around 6 miles (10 kilometers) to the southwest stood the palace of the king. The common people lived in mud houses between these two sections of the town.

Niani

According to tradition, Sundiata made a small village called Niani into the capital of the Mali Empire in the 1200's. Good farmlands surrounded Niani. By the 1300's, Niani had grown into a center of trade and learning. Archaeologists have found the remains there of an **Arab** neighborhood, a royal household, foundations of stone houses, and a **mosque.** They have also found traces of neighborhoods devoted to various crafts, such as metalworking, weaving, fishing, and leatherworking.

Timbuktu

Timbuktu was founded in about 1100. It became an important center of trade and education in the 1300's as part of the Mali Empire. It reached its greatest importance as part of the Songhai Empire, after Emperor Sunni Ali conquered the city in 1468.

▲ Timbuktu was a center of trade and education during the Mali and Songhai empires, as it still is today.

Djenne

From the 1200's to the 1700's, Djenne was an important center of trade between the Timbuktu region and the gold-producing and **kola-nut**-producing lands to the south. The Mali emperors tried again and again to bring Djenne into the empire, but failed. Songhai Emperor Sunni Ali finally conquered the city in the 1470's. Djenne had a university that was a famous center for the study of law, **Islam,** and medicine.

Gao

The Songhai people founded Gao in the early 600's. The town became prosperous as a trade and market center. In the early 1000's, Gao became the capital of the Songhai people. The Arab travel writer Leo Africanus (AF *rih KAN uhs*) visited Gao in about 1510. He described it as a town full of prosperous merchants, though most of its houses were "poor and ugly." Gao remained a center of trade and culture until about 1600.

▲ Surrounded by water, the city of Djenne, in a contemporary image, was difficult for the Mali emperors to conquer.

THE LEADERS

In the West African empires, kings and other leaders usually came from a ruling **clan.** Leadership passed through the male side of the family.

The Cisse of Ghana

In Ghana, the king, government officials, and governors of the **provinces** were made up of people from a Soninke clan called the Cisse, or Sisse *(SIH sah)*. According to tradition, the Cisse was one of the original Soninke clans. The first Cisse was named Dyabe *(dee YAH beh)*. According to **legend,** his father was Dinga *(DIHN guh)* and his mother was said to be the daughter of a goblin. Through military conquest, Dyabe founded a kingdom. He divided the kingdom into four provinces. Each of the provinces was ruled by a commander. The offspring of Dinga and of the commanders became the noble clans of ancient Ghana.

GOD-KINGS

In some places and times in West Africa, the emperor was worshiped as a god. Thus, the people of Ghana did not believe the emperor needed to eat. Food was brought to the palace secretly. Any ordinary person who saw the food going into the palace was immediately put to death.

▼ A house in Djenne, made of **adobe,** is larger and grander than other houses in the city. A chief or leader would have lived in such a house.

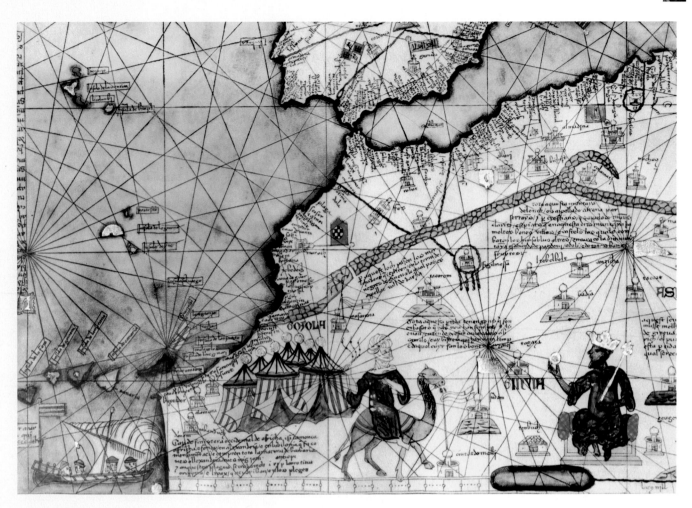

▲ A famous map of northern Africa, drawn by European mapmaker Abraham Cresques *(kres KEHZ)* in around 1375, shows Mansa Musa, who ruled the Mali Empire at its height, holding a piece of gold.

The Keitas of Mali

According to the **Arab** historian Ibn Khaldun, who lived in the 1300's, the first king of Mali was Barmandana *(bahr mahn DAHN uh)*, who ruled around 1050. Ibn Khaldun wrote that Barmandana became a **Muslim** and was the first of the Malian kings to make the **pilgrimage** to Mecca. After that time, the rulers of the empires of Mali (and later, Songhai) were Muslims.

The Keitas were the ruling clan of the Malian empire. According to Mande oral tradition, the Keitas were Muslim long before Barmandana. The Mandes believe their ancestors were descended from a companion of the prophet Muhammad,

the founder of **Islam**. Tradition states that this companion moved from Mecca, the Islamic holy city, to West Africa sometime in the 600's.

The Muslim Leaders of Songhai

Sunni Ali, who ruled from 1464 to 1492, founded the Songhai Empire. Although he was officially a Muslim, he also followed a traditional African religion. The ordinary people considered him almost a god. Songhai's next great leader, Askia Muhammad, ruled as a strict Muslim. But he did not want to offend the ordinary people by ignoring their traditions. He appointed the chief priest of the Songhai people to a high office in his government.

SUNDIATA, THE LION KING OF MALI

▲ Thatched houses in the town of Kirina, in present-day Mali, where Sundiata is said to have defeated the Soso king Sumanguru in about 1235.

The story of Sundiata, the founder of the Mali Empire, is part **legend** and part fact. What is known is that Sundiata was king of Kangaba. He led his people in a war of independence against the Soso people. The war ended in a victory for Sundiata at the Battle of Kirina *(kih REE nuh)*. Then Sundiata expanded the Mali Empire through a series of military victories. He ruled well, successfully blending **Islamic** and traditional African beliefs.

Sundiata's Youth

There are several versions of the legend of Sundiata. According to one version, Sundiata was the son of King Nare Maghan's *(nah ray mah GAHN)* second wife, Sogolon *(soh goh LOHN)*, who was a hunchback. Sundiata was born disabled and could not walk. When Sundiata was 3 years old, the king died. The 11-year-old son of the king's first, or chief, wife was heir to the throne. The chief wife ruled in her son's place as queen mother. The queen mother constantly mocked Sundiata.

When Sundiata was 7 years old, he miraculously got up and walked. He grew strong and soon became a master hunter.

SUNDIATA'S FAMILY
Sundiata's family, the Keita **clan,** claimed that they were descended from Bilali Bounama *(boo nah MAH),* a companion of Muhammad. Bilali is said to have been Islam's first muezzin *(myoo EHZ uhn),* the person who calls **Muslims** to prayer. According to tradition, Bilali, or one of his sons, moved from Mecca to West Africa. Bilali's descendants are credited with bringing Islam to Africa.

The queen mother did not want Sundiata to threaten her son's position. She tried to have Sundiata killed. Sogolon fled with Sundiata and her two daughters. Several years later, Kangaba came under the power of the cruel tyrant Sumanguru *(soo mahn GOO roo),* king of the Soso. Sumanguru conquered the kingdom. He forced Sundiata's half-brother, the king of Kangaba, to flee.

Warrior King

Sundiata raised an army and rode out to fight Sumanguru. Both Sundiata and Sumanguru were powerful sorcerers. During the battle, Sundiata fought with clever battle strategy. But Sumanguru escaped him by magically vanishing and reappearing elsewhere. Sundiata learned that the secret to overcoming Sumanguru's magic power was the spur, or back claw, of a white rooster. Sundiata hit Sumanguru in the arm with an arrow tipped with a rooster's spur. Sumanguru's power left him instantly, and he fled into a cave, never to be seen again.

The lesser rulers in the Soso kingdom recognized Sundiata as their ruler. He set up his capital at Niani. Sundiata ruled fairly, and the people lived in peace and prosperity.

▶ Actor Josh Tower plays Simba in Disney's Broadway musical *The Lion King.* The musical and the earlier animated film of the same name were based in part upon the Sundiata legend. In the Disney telling, a young lion named Simba rises to kingship on the African savanna, despite great obstacles.

LIFE AT COURT

In the days of the Ghana Empire, most **court** ceremonies were based on traditional African ways. This continued to be the case in Mali and Songhai, even though the rulers had converted to **Islam** by the time these empires flourished. Eventually, however, Islam began to hold a stronger influence on life in the royal courts of the West African empires.

The Splendor of the Court

According to the geographer al-Bakri, the emperor of Ghana received citizens at his palace surrounded by members of his court and government officials. Such meetings were announced with the beating of a drum. Al-Bakri described **pages** holding golden shields and swords. Captive princes—sons of lesser kings of the empire—with golden thread woven into their hair, stood at the king's side. Dogs with collars made from silver and gold guarded the entrance.

In the 1300's, a famous **Arab** traveler and writer, Ibn Battuta *(IHB uhn bat TOO tah)*, described a similar ceremony at the court of the emperor of Mali. He said that meetings with the emperor took place on a platform under a tree near the palace. The platform was covered in silk and cushions and shaded by a silk umbrella. The emperor walked from the palace to the platform to the sound of drums and the music of horns and two-stringed guitars. The emperor was dressed in red velvet and wore a skullcap of gold. Three hundred armed slaves guarded him. Helpers brought out two saddled horses. They also brought out two goats—believed to protect the emperor against evil spells.

▼ Earrings of gold, from present-day Mali, are similar to those that would have been worn in earlier times. Gold was the foundation of the wealth of the **medieval** West African emperors, and they and the people at their courts would have adorned themselves with golden jewelry.

Greeting the King

The West African rulers played a very active part in running their empires. They regularly allowed citizens to speak to them directly about problems. Throughout the Ghana, Mali, and Songhai empires, there was a similar **ritual** for approaching the emperor. Citizens had to fall face down before him, slap their chest, and throw dust and ashes over their head.

◀ An artist's depiction of a scene described by Ibn Battuta at the court of the emperor of Mali. The emperor is shaded from the sun by a silk umbrella, while being carried on a litter by his attendants.

WARRIORS

The empires of West Africa grew by means of warfare. Professional soldiers were also used to keep order throughout the **provinces** and defend against enemies. For these reasons, warriors held honored positions in **medieval** West African society. The kingdoms that formed the Ghana Empire gained power because they were better warriors and knew how to fight on horseback. This enabled them to conquer neighboring kingdoms whose warriors were not as well equipped or trained.

From the time of the Ghana Empire onward, the rulers used cavalries—that is, army units mounted on horseback. Soldiers on horseback could attack quickly and suddenly. Their unprepared enemies often had little or no chance to fight back.

▲ An iron sculpture of a horse and a rider with bow and arrows made by the Dogon *(DOH gon)* people, who lived within the Mali Empire. Such sculptures, called altar irons, were placed on the altars of family shrines dedicated to ancestors.

Volunteer Armies

The emperors of Mali and Ghana commanded large armies with skilled cavalries. But these armies were primarily made up of volunteers. In times of war, the rulers of Ghana and Mali raised armies made up of farmers and other ordinary men. When the fighting was over, these soldiers went back to their regular lives.

The army commanders, however, were paid well. In Ghana, some soldiers served as royal bodyguards, advisers, and escorts. These men were given their assignments based on character and skill.

THE VALUE OF HORSES

Horses were so important in maintaining power in the West African empires that they became symbols of high status. African rulers often traded slaves for horses. According to tradition, the ruler of Ghana had 1,000 horses. Richly saddled and bridled horses were always present during court ceremonies in Ghana and Mali.

In Mali, cavalry commanders were important members of the **court**. The emperor rewarded them with gifts of slaves, gold, horses, fine clothes, and even villages. The most able of these commanders got gold ankle bracelets and wide-legged trousers—the wider the leg of the trouser, the more honored the commander. Lower-ranked citizens supported the commanders. Farmers produced food for them, blacksmiths made their swords and other weapons, and leatherworkers crafted their saddles.

The Professional Army of Songhai

In the 1490's, the Songhai Emperor Askia Muhammad formed a full-time, professional army. He was probably the first West African leader to do so. The emperor could send troops to fight wherever they were needed at any time. Askia Muhammad also formed a professional navy that fought from war canoes.

▶ A clay statue, dating from the 1200's or 1300's, shows a richly clothed man on horseback. The sculpture may represent a professional warrior of the Mali Empire.

TRADERS

Because of the importance of trade in the West African empires, merchants and traders held a high position in society. Many of them became fabulously wealthy by running long-distance trade across the Sahara. They used camel **caravans** to transport goods across the desert.

The Dyula and Tuareg

In the Ghana and Mali empires, merchants and traders were mostly **Muslims**. The Mande people called them **Dyula** *(dih YOO luh)*, a Mande word that means "traveling trader." The Dyula were among the first West Africans to convert to **Islam**. The Dyula belonged to the Mande **ethnic group.** They controlled the gold fields in what are now Guinea and Cote d'Ivoire *(koht dee VWAR)*, also known as Ivory Coast. The Dyula held power because they knew the secret locations of the gold fields.

The Dyula were important traders throughout West Africa. Originally, their main goods were gold, salt, and **kola nuts.** But by the 1300's, they traded many goods, including beads, cloth, copper, glass, ivory, and silver. The Dyula dealt with another group of traders, the **Tuareg.** The Tuareg brought such goods as salt to the south. The Tuareg would trade with the Dyula for such things as gold and kola nuts, and then travel to their homes in the north.

▲ Tuareg traders in modern-day Timbuktu load a camel with salt in preparation for a caravan trip. Traders have used this method of transporting goods across the Sahara for centuries.

▲ A sign informs travelers in both French and Arabic that it will take 52 days to reach Timbuktu.

Dyula Society

The Dyula settled throughout the cities of the West African empires. They often gathered in their own neighborhoods, which were separate from the non-Muslim people. Dyula **clans** were divided into two kinds. Clans called tun digi (*tuhn DIH gee*) had their roots in the warrior class. The mory (*MOH ree*) clans were traditionally Islamic scholars. However, membership in any given clan did not determine what a Dyula's job might be.

LANGUAGE OF TRADE

Trade in kola nuts and salt was so important to the Dyula that their language was shaped by it. Their word for "south" was worodugu (*woh roh doo GOO*), or "the land of kola," and their word for "north" was kogodugu (*koh goh doo GOO*), or "the land of salt."

FARMERS

▲ A woman in present-day Mali farms her plot of land in the fertile soil near the Niger River. Farming practices in the area have remained the same for centuries.

Most of the people of the West African empires tended crops. They grew such grains as millet, rice, and sorghum, as well as okra *(OH kruh)*, yams, and other vegetables. They also grew melons and peanuts and raised cattle, sheep, and goats.

Farming Skills

Historians believe that people were farming the area around the **delta** of the Niger River by at least 500 B.C. A delta is the triangular-shaped area of rich soil deposited at the mouth of a river. Farmers probably planted rice in the rich soil left behind when floodwaters drained away after the rainy season. As early as 1000 B.C., the people of West Africa had become skilled farmers. They built dikes and small dams to collect water for their crops. They probably grew more than enough food for their communities and were able to trade it for other goods they needed.

Horonnu

In the culture of the Mande people of the Mali Empire, the farmers made up a **caste** called the horonnu *(hohr oh noo)*. The horonnu had high status in Mande society. Besides farming, horonnu served in the government and

Behaving properly was very important in the cultures of West Africa. Behavior that was acceptable for one caste was not acceptable for others. The horonnu were expected to behave properly at all times because of their high caste. They saw the artisans as wild and shameless. For example, the horonnu would not play certain musical instruments or dance as traditional musicians, called **griots,** *(gree OHZ)* did.

the military. They also were hunters. Emperors and other rulers generally were from the horonnu caste. The horonnu supported the **artisans,** who were of a lower caste. In exchange for the goods and services artisans provided, the horonnu gave the artisans food or money.

Although farmers were a high-status caste in the West African empires, most farmers were not rich. They lived modest, though comfortable, lives. The farms were small—less than 10 acres (4 hectares)—in the West African kingdoms. Farmers lived in small houses made of **adobe** or stone and wood. Each person had a cot or mat to sleep on, but there was little other furniture. Because of the hot climate, people carried on most activities outdoors.

▶ Following a farming practice that is centuries old, present-day farmers throughout the **Sahel** store crops under a thatched granary *(GRAN uhr ee)* supported on a raised platform. The granary keeps out pests.

ARTISANS

People who make beautiful and useful objects are known as
artisans. In **medieval** West African societies, artisans were of
fairly low status. At the same time, they were greatly respected—and
sometimes feared—because they were believed to have magical
powers.

Nyamakalalu

Artisans belonged to a **social class** called **nyamakalalu** *(nih YAH mah
kah lah LOO)*. Among the Mande people, artisans were thought to
have special control over **nyama** *(nih YAH mah)*. In West African
belief, nyama is the powerful and dangerous life energy that runs
through all things. Artisans needed this special control and power
because the materials they worked with—iron and other metals, clay,
leather, and wood—were thought to have especially strong nyama.
Nyamakalalu were believed to be born with the ability to pursue their
craft in safety from nyama.

Nyamakalalu made such useful everyday items as iron tools,
pottery, and saddles. But they also made important **ritual** objects,
such as leather cases for charms, drums, and wooden masks used in
ceremonies. Nyamakalalu would preside over important rituals and
cast spells. People thought the nyamakalalu could see into the future.

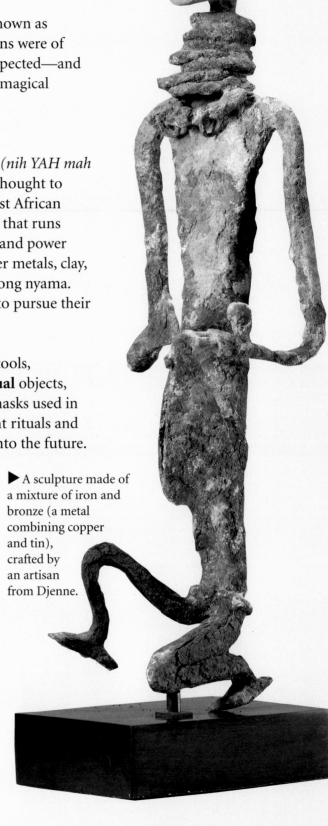

▶ A sculpture made of
a mixture of iron and
bronze (a metal
combining copper
and tin),
crafted by
an artisan
from Djenne.

WEAVERS AND TAILORS
Spinning and weaving probably started
in West Africa in around the A.D. 900's.
Before that, most clothing was probably
made of leather. The cloth industry in the
West African empires started in the 1000's.
It reached its peak in the 1400's and
1500's. Some weavers were in the artisan
caste and ranked just below blacksmiths.
Others were **Muslims** who were outside
the caste system. High-status Muslims
worked as weavers and tailors in Timbuktu and Djenne. At one point in the
1600's, there were 26 weaving and
tailoring workshops in Timbuktu. Each
one employed 50 to 100 **apprentices**
(uh PREHN tihs uhz).

◀ A blacksmith in Niger uses traditional methods to forge iron. The skills of the blacksmith have been highly prized in West Africa for hundreds of years.

Blacksmiths

The West Africans believed that, among artisans, blacksmiths had especially strong magical powers. Blacksmiths made tools, weapons, and other items from iron. To shape iron, they used very hot fires to melt the ore. Then they hammered the hot iron into the desired shape. The West Africans believed these activities released a huge amount of nyama.

Blacksmiths kept their ironworking skills a secret. They set up groups called lodges. Only those who were experts in the secret skills of ironworking could be members. Blacksmith lodges were responsible for repairing roads and bridges in the Mali Empire. In this way they had some control over trade and travel in the empire.

GRIOTS

Griots were musicians, storytellers, and keepers of the oral history of West Africa. They often played an important role in traditional African societies that had languages without a written form. In many West African societies, griots made up a low-ranking **caste.** In spite of their low rank, they were greatly respected and feared. Like blacksmiths, griots were part of the **nyamakalalu** caste. Griots were usually men.

Traveling Entertainers

Some griots were simply entertainers who traveled alone. They created songs, poems, and chants for public and private events and played a stringed instrument called the kora *(KAWR uh)*. They did not have any special status in society.

▼ The balafon, which was played by the griots, is an ancient West African instrument that is still played today.

A modern-day griot in Mali plays the kora, a stringed instrument.

Dyelis of Mali

In Mali, some griots served as counselors and companions to rulers. These griots were called dyelis *(dih YEHL eez)*. The dyeli was often the emperor's most trusted friend. The dyeli had several responsibilities.

The dyeli directed music and dance performances for the emperor. The **Arab** traveler and writer Ibn Battuta described a ceremony performed every Friday afternoon after prayers in the Mali capital. The ceremony began with the dyeli appearing before the emperor. Also in attendance were the emperor's wives and female slaves. The women, playing bowed instruments, sang along with the dyeli. The dyeli played the balafon *(BAHL uh fohn)*, an instrument similar to a xylophone. Then poets joined the ceremony, dressed in masks with feathers and red beaks. The poets recited the histories of the rulers of Mali and reminded the king that he should rule wisely and well.

The dyeli also acted as the emperor's public spokesman. The dyeli, holding a pair of spears, would repeat the emperor's official announcements so that all could hear. It was also the dyeli's job to settle quarrels between groups.

SLAVES

▲ Iron shackles *(SHAK uhlz)* used to bind the feet of slaves.

Slavery was part of life in the West African kingdoms. Slavery took many forms, and there were a number of ways that people could become enslaved. People captured in warfare were sometimes enslaved. Criminals could be punished with slavery. Some people repaid their debts with a period of slavery. Children born to enslaved parents were also slaves. **Arabs** and Africans from the north raided remote villages. The raiders sold captives to Arab traders north of the Sahara.

Not all types of slaves were enslaved their entire life. Those enslaved to pay off debt could be freed when they had worked off the amount they owed. According to tradition, some slaves had certain rights. For example, slave owners faced severe punishment for mistreating household slaves.

The Work of Slaves

Some enslaved men were put to work on farms. Others worked as bodyguards. Young women were sometimes enslaved to serve as household servants or as companions to rulers and wealthy men.

Other slaves toiled under terrible conditions. Such slaves were used as porters, or carriers, of goods. They carried heavy loads of gold and salt on their heads on long treks. Slaves worked in the salt mines and copper mines. Such slaves were often beaten and were sometimes worked to death.

▼ An illustration from the early 1800's shows chained African captives bound for the slave trade.

Powerful Slaves

Slaves who worked as household servants could have close relationships with their masters. They were sometimes given much responsibility, and some married into their master's family. Some slaves in the emperor's household had great power, even more power than people of high birth. Mansa Musa's most trusted servant was the slave who ran his household. The chief financial officer of the city of Walata was a slave. His title was mansa-dyon *(MAHN sah di YOHN)*, or the "king's slave." Mansa Sakuru, who became emperor of Mali in about 1300, was a freed slave. He ruled well and helped the kingdom regain some of its strength after a period of weakness.

LAW AND ORDER

Law and order were strong in the Mali, Ghana, and Songhai empires. Because of the importance of trade in the empires, many laws existed to protect traders, travelers, and property. In Ghana, the emperor played a direct role in the justice system. He would ride through the streets every morning, hearing the complaints of citizens. He would not return to his palace until the problems he was asked about were solved.

Protecting Merchants

If a **Muslim** died in Mali, the government made sure all his property was protected until it was claimed by the deceased person's heirs. Foreign merchants who thought they had been cheated or mistreated could take their complaints directly to the emperor. Once a trader appeared before Mansa Suleyman *(SOO luh MAHN* or *SOO lay MAHN)* of Mali and accused a government official in the town of Walata of underpaying him. Suleyman brought the official to the capital, where he was ordered to pay the merchant what was owed him. The official was fired from his job.

In Mali, theft was such a serious crime that those convicted were sentenced to death or slavery. As a result, society was quite orderly. **Arab** traveler and writer Ibn Battuta claimed that he traveled alone with only one guide. Women could travel with great amounts of gold jewelry without fear of being robbed.

▲ A woman in modern-day Mali wearing jewelry of gold and amber beads. People in **medieval** Mali also wore gold and other valuables without fear.

Islamic Law

By the time of the Songhai Empire, **Islam** had spread further. **Ulamas** *(OO luh MAHZ)*, or scholars in the religion and law of Islam, had more power in the Songhai Empire, and Islamic law became stronger.

▼ Pages from an ancient Qur'an *(ku RAHN)*, sometimes spelled Koran, are preserved in a library in present-day Mauritania. The Islamic scriptures formed the basis of the law in the time of the Songhai Empire.

TRADITIONAL LAW IN GHANA

Ghana was not influenced much by Islamic law. According to the geographer al-Bakri, people accused of a crime were judged by a tradition called *trial by wood*. The accused had to drink a bitter potion made with the sap from the wood of a particular tree. If the person vomited, he or she was considered innocent.

Ghana had special military forces whose duty was to keep order. They were armed with spears, daggers, swords, war clubs, and bows and arrows. They wore uniforms and lived in compounds.

TRADITIONAL BELIEFS AND GODS

Traditional West African religions began before the Sahara started turning to desert, which was about 4,000 years ago. In this early time, people worshiped nature gods that were identified with such animals as the ram and the python. Rulers had to be priests or sorcerers because the people believed that such rulers received their powers from a god or gods. These powers were transferred to a ruler through his ancestors.

Ancestor worship formed part of many African **mythologies.** Many Africans believed, and in some places still believe, that after death the souls of their ancestors are reborn in living things or in objects. Magic also played a major role in traditional religions. Priests had great influence among many African peoples because the priests were believed to have magical powers. Many Africans wore charms to protect themselves from harm.

THE SACRED GROVES OF KUMBI SALEH

According to the scholar and geographer Al-Bakri, there were sacred groves in the emperor's town in Kumbi Saleh. These woods were the home of the sorcerers, the storage place for idols (statues representing gods), and the burial place for kings.

◄ Traditional West African religions made use of charms and spells. Shirts covered in charms were used in religious rituals.

Gods and Spirits

Many West African peoples believed in a supreme god that did not interfere in everyday human affairs. This god had different names among different peoples. The Mande people believed this supreme god created the world by speaking. Other spirits lived in nature, including the earth, the water, plants, and animals. These gods both helped and hurt human beings.

Use of Magic

The use of **ritual** magic and spells was widespread in the West African empires. Sorcerers put spells on other people and used charms to protect themselves. The **Arab** historian al-Umari *(ahl OO mahr EE),* writing in the 1300's, described how the Mali people would ask the emperor for help when someone used magic against their families. They would say, "So-and-so killed my brother by magic, or my son, or my sister, or my daughter." Al-Umari said that sorcerers were put to death based on such accusations.

Each **caste—artisans,** warriors, farmers, hunters, and slaves—had its own spiritual practices. They made charms to protect themselves from foreign spirits. Traditional beliefs in Mali were based on **nyama,** which they regarded as a powerful life force that ran throughout the world. Blacksmiths and masons, those who work with stone and brick, were thought to have the most power to control nyama.

▶ According to tradition, the founders of the Ghana Empire were helped by a snake god called Wagadu-Bida *(WAHG uh DOO BEE dah).* The snake on the forehead of this clay figure from the Mali Empire in the 1400's could show that Wagadu-Bida continued to be an important god in the traditional religions of the West African empires.

ISLAM

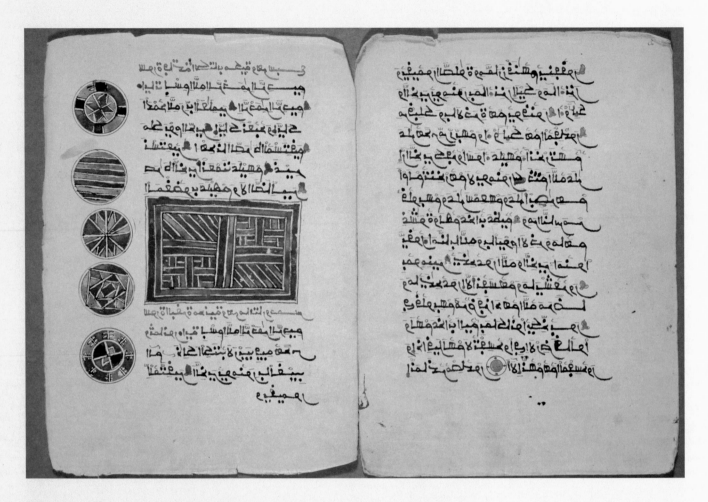

I**slam** began to take hold in West Africa in the mid-700's. **Arab** traders from North Africa spread Islam in West African cities. In the Ghana Empire, Islam was not very widespread, though some rulers were reported to be **Muslims**. The African traders called **Dyula** were probably among the first to adopt Islam.

Islam in Mali and Songhai

In the 1300's, at the height of the Mali Empire, Islam was strong in the cities and among the ruling and merchant classes. Mansa Musa, Mansa Suleyman, and other emperors of Mali were officially Muslims. However, these rulers still followed many traditional religious practices. Arab traveler and writer Ibn Battuta wrote that Islamic festivals were big events in the Mali capital. The emperor arrived at the place of prayer on horseback with red silk flags flying. Muslim officials followed the emperor, while calling out "Allah is great!" Prayers, a sermon, and a speech followed.

▲ A beautifully illuminated (*ih LOO muh NAY tihd*), or decorated, Qur'an that was created in West Africa in the A.D. 1700's. Islam has continued in importance in West Africa through the centuries since the West African empires.

By the time of the Songhai Empire, Islam was better established, though it still was centered more in the cities than in the countryside. Emperor Askia Muhammad, a Muslim, set up the government according to the principles of Islam.

Pilgrimage to Mecca

Under Islam, every healthy adult who is financially able is required to journey to Mecca at least once in his or her life. Some of the emperors of Ghana, Mali, and Songhai made the **pilgrimage.** Mansa Musa's pilgrimage in 1324 became legendary throughout the Islamic world for the huge amount of gold he gave away.

▲ Imams *(ih MAHMZ)*, or Muslim religious leaders, in a **mosque** in modern-day Mali. West Africans began to convert to Islam in the A.D. 700's.

ROOTS OF ISLAM

Islam began in the early A.D. 600's with the teachings of the prophet Muhammad. Followers of Islam believe that in about 610, Muhammad began to receive revelations from Allah (God) that were transmitted by the angel Gabriel. These revelations took place over about a 22-year period in the cities of Mecca and Medina *(muh DEE nuh)*. Both cities are in present-day Saudi Arabia. The revelations were assembled in a book called the Qur'an.

MOSQUES

M ost of the larger towns and cities of the Mali and Songhai empires had more than one **mosque**. The mosques were a blend of traditional West African and North African building materials and styles. In North Africa, the mosques were made of stone or baked-mud bricks and had tall, thin **minarets** (MIHN *uh REHTZ*). Some West African mosques were made of packed clay. The minarets were often short and cone-shaped, similar to the cone-shaped clay houses of African villages.

Djenne Mosque

In about 1240, the Malian ruler Koi *(koh ee)* Kunboro ordered that his palace in Djenne should be converted into a mosque. It was a very large building, constructed entirely of mud brick and mud plaster. This mosque stood until the early 1800's. Another mosque was built on the site in the early 1900's (see illustration on page 4).

▼ The Jingereber Mosque in Timbuktu was built in the 1300's.

Mansa Musa's Mosques

In the 1300's, Emperor Mansa Musa ordered the building of mosques throughout the Mali Empire. Mansa Musa built a mud mosque in Timbuktu, called Jingereber *(JIHN gehr eh buhr)*, that was designed by a Spanish architect. Jingereber, which still stands, has high walls, a flat roof, and nine rows of square pillars. It can hold as many as 2,000 worshipers.

Mansa Musa also built a mosque in Gao. Only the foundation of the Gao Mosque remains.

Sankore Mosque

The Sankore *(SAN kohr eh)* Mosque in Timbuktu was built sometime between the early 1300's and the mid-1400's, when the city was part of the Mali Empire. The mosque is made of mud brick and of a type of hard clay cut into squares, called Timbuktu stone. The mosque's large pyramid-shaped mihrab *(MEE ruhb)* makes Sankore different from other mosques. A mihrab is a decorative arch in the inner wall of a mosque that shows the direction of the holy city Mecca, which **Muslims** face for their daily prayers. The Sankore Mosque still stands.

▲ The Sankore Mosque in Timbuktu was built sometime in the 1300's or 1400's. The wooden beams sticking out are used by maintenance workers to climb the walls.

MAINTAINING MOSQUES

Heavy downpours during the rainy season wash away the mud plaster that covers and protects the **adobe** bricks from which many mosques in West Africa are built. As a result, the walls must be re-covered in mud every year. To make this easier, builders placed wooden beams into some mosque walls. The beams stick out a few feet. Workers use the beams to climb up the walls and replace the mud.

TOMBS AND BURIALS

Information on tombs and burials from the time of the Ghana, Mali, and Songhai empires comes from both written descriptions and evidence found by **archaeologists**. In the **Sahel**, burials were in tomblike hills of earth called burial mounds. In other areas, people were buried "curled up" in large ceramic urns—vases or vaselike containers. **Muslims** have rules against disturbing gravesites, so Muslim burials have not been widely studied by researchers.

MARBLE TOMBSTONES
Many Muslim cemeteries dating from the 1100's to the 1300's have been found near Gao. These cemeteries contain tombstones made of marble imported from Spain. Inscriptions on some of the tombstones are in an early form of Arabic. Some of the tombstones mark the graves of Songhai kings.

▼ The tomb of Askia Muhammad, in Gao, is built in a traditional style of West Africa. Askia Muhammad ruled the Songhai Empire from 1493 to 1528.

▼ In some areas of West Africa, people were buried in large pottery urns. A burial urn dating from the 1400's (below) was found in a burial mound in Djenne.

Burial Mounds

Archaeologists have found remains of three different types of burial mounds throughout the region. From the 100's B.C. to the A.D. 900's, Saharan peoples buried their dead in stone burial mounds. Peoples of the dry savanna regions east and west of the Niger **Delta** buried their dead in earthen burial mounds. In the forested savanna regions, some tombs were cut from rock that was buried under mounds of earth.

Burial mounds varied in size, depending on the person's wealth and power. The tombs of rulers and wealthy people were large. Some of them had a hard covering that was created by burning many fires on a layer of clay. Others had a wooden chamber inside with a shaft leading to the top of the mound.

The Spanish-**Arab** scholar and geographer Al-Bakri describes how rulers of Ghana were buried: "When the king dies, they build a huge dome of wood over the burial place. Then they bring him on a bed lightly covered, and put him inside the dome. At his side they place his ornaments, his arms [weapons] and the vessels from which he used to eat and drink, filled with food and beverages. They bring in those men who used to serve his food and drink. Then they close the door of the dome and cover it with mats and other materials. People gather and pile earth over it until it becomes like a large mound."

Stone Circles

The ruins of about 2,000 ancient cemeteries that include circles of large stones and earthen burial mounds have been found in present-day Senegal and Gambia. Archaeologists believe that various groups of ancient peoples built the tombs between 200 B.C. and A.D. 1500. Scientists think that some may contain the remains of rulers of the Mali Empire. The stones range in size from about 3 feet (1 meter) to 10 feet (3 meters) tall. Some tombs contain the remains of one person. Others contain the remains of 30 or more people.

FAMILY LIFE

The extended family—including grandparents, aunts and uncles, and cousins—was central to life in the West African empires. In Ghana, the people lived in small farming villages made up of several large family groups. People in Mali also lived in extended family groups. Such groups were called lus *(luhs)*. The head of the family was called the fa *(fah)*. He was in charge of the family's property and ruled over relationships within the group. He also had religious responsibilities. The organization of family and village life was similar in Mali and Songhai.

Husbands and Wives

Men were allowed to have more than one wife in the West African empires. But, because they had to support their wives and their children, it is likely that only rulers and wealthy men had multiple wives. **Muslim** men were limited to four wives. Men could easily divorce their wives for any reason. Women had no voice in choosing their husband.

The emperor of Mali had a senior wife. She was usually of noble birth. Her name was announced along with the emperor's in public ceremonies.

▼ Young girls in Mali pound grain to grind it into flour. In West Africa today, as in the past, children are expected to help with many tasks.

The emperor also had a large harem *(HAIR uhm)*, or group of women who lived with him but had lower status than his wives. Songhai emperors often chose the daughters of their military officers to be in their harem. During the 1500's, all the emperors of Songhai were sons of women from the harem.

Children

Children in the Mali Empire spent most of their time with their mothers until they were 12 years old. At that time, the boys went through a ceremony marking their entrance into manhood. Most boys then began training in a craft with their uncles. A few went to study in the city. Others joined the military. Girls were considered to be adults at about the same age as were boys. Once she reached adulthood, a girl was usually married to a man of her father's choosing.

THE IMPORTANCE OF NAMES

In the Mali culture, a person's family, or last, name was inherited from the father. Children were taught from an early age to live according to the traditions of the father's family. The given, or first, name stood for personal achievements. Sometimes a son was named by putting his mother's given name before the family name. Emperor Sundiata's name was a shortened form of his mother's given name, Sogolon, and his family name, Diata, which meant "lion."

▲ A bronze sculpture of a husband and wife made by the Dogon people in Mali.

SHELTER AND CLOTHING

Shelter and clothing in the **medieval** West African empires differed between the people of the cities and the people of the countryside, between the rich and powerful and the poor, and between **Muslims** and those following traditional African ways of life.

Shelter

According to **Arab** travel writer Leo Africanus, in Djenne in the early 1500's, the houses of "the king, the men of religion, the doctors of learning, the merchants and those of wealth and authority . . . were made like huts, of clay and thatched straw." Such homes were traditionally circular. Arab historian al-Umari, writing in the 1300's, described the houses in Niani, the capital of Mali, similarly.

▲ Many people in West Africa still live in thatched huts, as people did in the medieval West African empires.

HOMES OF SALT
People often build houses using materials that are readily available in their environment. In one salt-mining town in West Africa, people lived in homes built of salt blocks. They used camel hides to cover the roof.

Al-Bakri described the royal houses of Kumbi Saleh, in Ghana, as made of stone and wood. The king's palace was surrounded by circular huts. During the Songhai Empire, the king had a palace at Gao protected by a high wall. His wives and children lived in a separate palace. During the Ghana and Mali empires, Arab merchants and traders built rectangular houses of stone or brick. Some were even two stories high. Families lived in the top floor. The lower floor was used to store goods.

▼ Mud cloth is still woven in Mali today.

Clothing

The hot weather in West Africa meant that clothing was not needed for warmth. In the countryside, people might wear very little clothing or no clothing at all. In the **courts** of Mali and Ghana, people might sometimes appear in public wearing no clothing. Because nudity was against the laws of **Islam**, however, those people who dealt with Muslim traders wore clothing out of respect for the traders' beliefs.

Al-Bakri said that in the Ghana Empire, the Arabs wore sewn clothing, but among the African people only the emperor and his heir could wear sewn clothing. All others could wear only pieces of cloth wrapped around their bodies. The emperor of Mali wore luxurious clothing imported from Europe. The wealthy people of Walata wore imported Egyptian clothing.

In Mali, mud cloth, made by women, was used for clothing worn during birth, death, and marriage ceremonies. Mud cloth is a woven fabric that is soaked in a solution made from pounded leaves. This process gives the cloth a deep yellow color. The cloth is then decorated using a dye made from black mud collected from ponds.

EDUCATION

In the countryside during the time of the West African empires, there was little formal education. Young people learned about correct behavior, trades, healing, religion, and local government from their families.

Higher Learning

In the cities, where **Islam** played a larger role, there were opportunities for higher learning. Timbuktu and Gao were centers for Islamic scholarship. **Muslim** universities in West Africa were made up of several separate schools. Each of the schools was run by an imam, or religious leader. Students, all male, studied with an imam in the courtyard of the **mosque** or at the imam's house. Students learned Islamic religion and law, as well as nonreligious subjects.

Timbuktu had many private libraries. One scholar and author, Ahmed Baba *(AH mehd BAH bah)*, who lived in the late 1500's during the Songhai period, is said to have owned 1,600 books.

Sankore

Timbuktu began to rise as a center of Islamic learning after the reign of emperor Mansa Musa of Mali. Musa visited Timbuktu in the early 1300's and ordered a mosque to be built there. The mosque, called Sankore, included a university. Mansa Musa brought religious scholars from Cairo's al-Azhar *(ahl ah ZAHR)* University, which still exists today, to teach at Sankore. He also sent African **ulamas** to the Moroccan

▲ A page from an Islamic manuscript from the 1400's. Many such manuscripts are found in libraries in Timbuktu.

TIMBUKTU MANUSCRIPTS

After the fall of the Songhai Empire, Timbuktu began to decline as a center of learning. Today, as many as 700,000 original handwritten documents, called manuscripts *(MAN yuh skrihptz)*, from Timbuktu still exist. They cover a variety of subjects and are housed in various institutions and private collections around Timbuktu.

However, these precious manuscripts are in great danger. Some are being sold illegally. Others are slowly crumbling away. A private organization, the Timbuktu Heritage Institute, works to preserve and protect these ancient manuscripts.

city of Fez to study. During the 1300's and 1400's, thousands of young Africans studied such subjects as science, religion, geography, medicine, math, history, and law in a 10-year program at Sankore.

▼ An Islamic school in present-day Timbuktu.

TRANSPORTATION

People and goods traveled extensively throughout the West African empires. People used canoes to sail along the Niger from the empires' earliest times. By the late 700's, traders used camels to take goods across the Sahara Desert, between North Africa and West Africa. Camels and other animals carried merchants and traders and their goods long distances over land.

Transportation in Nondesert Areas

In nondesert areas, people used donkeys and oxen to transport goods and people. The military and rulers rode horses. But very few ordinary people used horses. Horses were for powerful and high-status people. A horse was quite expensive—costing four or five times more in Africa than in Europe. For these reasons, trade in horses was limited to the upper classes.

TSETSE FLIES

Horses and pack animals could not be used south of the savanna because of the tsetse *(TSEHT see)* fly. Tsetse flies cannot live in dry areas but thrive in the more humid forested regions. This insect spreads nagana *(nuh GAH nuh)*, a deadly disease of cattle and horses that in humans is called African sleeping sickness. The disease made pack animals unusable in the forest, so people carried loads on their heads.

▼ Travelers arrive in Timbuktu by camel, horse, and donkey in the 1850's. Transportation to Timbuktu in earlier times would have been much the same. The image is from *Travels and Discoveries in North and Central Africa, 1849-1855,* written by Heinrich Barth, a German explorer, and published in 1857.

Water Transportation

The Niger River was an important transportation route between the West African highlands and the Atlantic Ocean. Dugout canoes were used to transport slaves and paying passengers and such goods as gold, spices, cotton, ivory, and salt. Ferry services operated along the Niger. Coastal peoples also used these canoes on the ocean for trade and fishing, sometimes venturing hundreds of miles along the coast and up to 10 miles (16 kilometers) from shore.

In the Songhai Empire especially, canoes were important tools of government. During wartime, armies used canoes to transport troops. Battles were also fought between navies in canoes.

Some dugout canoes were 80 feet (25 meters) long and could carry 100 people. West Africans made such canoes from a single log. They hollowed out the log by carving, scraping, and burning. They powered the canoes by paddles, poles, and sometimes with sails.

▲ Traditional long, pointed canoes, like those employed during the Songhai Empire, are still used for transportation on the Niger River in Mali.

INVADERS CONQUER THE LAST GREAT AFRICAN EMPIRE

The Portuguese became the first Europeans to reach the coastal area of the West African empires in the 1440's. Eventually, the Europeans set up successful trading partnerships with the West African kingdoms. The Europeans got such raw materials as gold, ivory, and pepper, in exchange for such manufactured goods as metal tools, bowls, and utensils.

Muslim Invasions

Muslims from the north, including the **Tuareg** and Moroccans *(muh ROK uhnz)*, began attacking cities in the Songhai Empire in the 1500's. Songhai warriors were no match for the better-armed Moroccans, who carried a type of firearm called a **harquebus** *(HAHR kwuh buhs)*. The empire collapsed in 1591, when a Moroccan army defeated the Songhai in the Battle of Tondibi *(tohn dih bee)*.

During the same period, kingdoms within the empire that wanted independence began to rebel against the Songhai rulers. By 1650, all that was left of the Songhai Empire was a weak group of small kingdoms in the southeastern part of the once-great land.

▶An ivory salt container carved in West Africa in the 1500's. This container is carved in the style of the Benin people. Portuguese noblemen are shown on the base. On the lid is a type of Portuguese sailing ship, a caravel *(KAR uh vehl)*. The Portuguese used such ships to sail to Africa.

GETTING TO AFRICA

For hundreds of years, the civilizations of West Africa were protected from European invasion. Crossing the Sahara was too hard, and the west coast of Africa had few harbors for ships. In addition, northerly winds made it easy for ships to sail south along the coast, but difficult to sail north to return home. However, by the 1400's, the Portuguese and other Europeans had developed the sailing and shipbuilding skills necessary to make the round trip to and from the western coast of Africa.

▶ The Portuguese built Elmina Castle (in present-day Ghana) in 1482 to serve as a base for the gold trade. In 1637, Elmina Castle was captured by the Dutch and became a holding place for slaves before they were transported to North America.

The Slave Trade

After about 1625, the Europeans' interest turned to the slave trade. Europeans had set up plantations and mines in the Americas and needed cheap labor. And the Europeans had a product that the African rulers wanted—guns. Slaves were already used as a source of wealth in Africa. But, the European demand for slaves made the trade far more profitable than it had ever been before. The slave trade devastated West Africa. The kingdoms lost a large number of their people. Wars fought for captives led to ruin throughout the region. By the 1800's, Europeans had brought as many as 10 million slaves from western Africa to the Americas.

Gradually, European countries began to set up colonies throughout Africa. By 1914, nearly the whole of Africa was under European control.

THE LEGACY FROM THE EMPIRES OF GOLD

The region once controlled by the empires of Ghana, Mali, and Songhai now covers some or all of the countries of Burkina Faso, Gambia, Guinea, Mali, Mauritania, Niger, and Senegal. The splendor of the **medieval** kingdoms of gold is gone. But many aspects of life in this region have changed little in the passing centuries.

People in this region of West Africa still often live in small villages in close-knit communities made up of the same **ethnic group**. Many of these villagers still practice traditional ways of farming. Small boats are still used to move goods on the Niger River. **Caravans** may not be as common as they once were, and modern caravans may sometimes use motorcycles and trucks in place of camels, but traders still cross the Sahara today. It is possible to see women in Timbuktu wearing large amounts of gold jewelry, as they have for hundreds of years.

▼ People gather in a bustling marketplace in Djenne, an important center of trade for centuries.

▲ Accompanied by a kora player, singer Salif Keita performs at a concert in Senegal in 2005. Keita, an internationally known performer of Afropop, is descended from Sundiata Keita.

The greatest legacy of the West African empires comes to us through art. Stories from West Africa about a lion king or the trickster spider, Anansi *(ah NAHN see)*, are told around the world. **Griots** still perform in West Africa. Many modern musical forms, especially blues, jazz, rock-and-roll, and reggae, have their roots in traditional West African music. Masks, worn during **ritual** dramas, are also part of the heritage of African art. These art forms help West Africans feel connected to their ancestors in the medieval empires of gold.

GRIOTS TODAY

The tradition of the griots is still strong in West Africa. Griots continue to play such instruments as the kora and balafon. However, today's griots power up their musical performances with amplifiers and use modern materials, such as nylon strings, in their instruments. The Internet, CDs, radio, and television have introduced the griot's art to audiences beyond Africa.

GLOSSARY

adobe Brick made of clay baked in the sun.

Almoravids A **Muslim** people from northern Africa.

apprentice A person who learns a trade by working under the guidance of a skilled master.

Arab A group of people whose native language is Arabic and who share a common history and culture. These people would have lived in the Arabian Peninsula in ancient times.

archaeologist A scientist who studies the remains of past human cultures.

artisan A person skilled in some industry or trade.

Berber A person of northern Africa and the Sahara. The Berbers speak a language that experts call Tamazight. Many Berbers follow Arabic customs and traditions and almost all Berbers are **Muslims.**

caravan A large group of traders or merchants who travel together.

caste In traditional African societies, a social group based not upon birth, but instead upon the type of trade a group practices. Often, individuals follow the trade their family practices.

civil service Professional people who are appointed by rulers, and not elected, to run the government.

clan A group of people who are related through a common ancestor.

court The place where a king or emperor lives; also, the family, household, or followers of a king or emperor.

delta A low plain composed of clay, sand, gravel, and other sediments deposited at the mouth of a river.

Dyula A Mande word meaning "traveling trader." Most Dyula in the West African empires were **Muslim** merchants and traders.

ethnic group A group of people with characteristics in common that distinguish them from most other people of the same society. Members may have ties of ancestry, culture, language, nationality, or religion, or a combination of these things.

griot A traditional musician, storyteller, and keeper of history in West Africa.

harquebus (also spelled arquebus) An early firearm. The weapon was invented in Spain and was used before muskets were invented.

Islam A major world religion begun in the A.D. 600's by the Prophet Muhammad.

kola nut The seed of several kinds of evergreen trees that are native to West Africa. This seed is chewed by Africans for its stimulating effect.

legend A folk story, often set in the past, which may be based in truth, but which may also contain fictional or fantastic elements. Legends are similar to myths, but myths often are about such sacred topics as gods or the creation of the world.

medieval Belonging to the period from around the A.D. 400's through the 1400's.

minaret A tower on a **mosque,** with a balcony from which a man calls the **Muslim** community to prayer.

mosque A building used for **Muslim** worship.

Muslim A follower of the religion of **Islam.**

mythology A body of sacred stories about such topics as gods and the creation of the world.

nomadic Moving from place to place in search of food.

nyama A life force or energy of nature. This force could be released when practicing certain crafts.

nyamakalalu A **caste** of **artisans** and artists in West Africa. Those of this class were believed to be able to safely control the life force, or life energy, called **nyama.**

page A boy who serves a king or other government official.

pilgrimage A journey made for religious reasons; **Muslims** who are able are required to make a pilgrimage once in their lives to **Islam's** holiest city, Mecca, in Saudi Arabia.

province A division of a kingdom, country, or empire.

ritual A solemn or important act or ceremony, often religious in nature.

Sahel A large, dry grassland in Africa located south of the Sahara and north of the rain forests.

siege Surrounding a city or fortified place with an army in order to capture the place.

social class A group of people who share a common status or position in society. Social classes represent differences in wealth, power, employment, family background, and other qualities.

Sudan A region of Africa that is south of the Sahara and north of the equator. A modern African country is also named Sudan, but this country lies east of the part of the Sudan region discussed here.

trade route A system of roads and pathways along which goods are transported.

Tuareg A group of nomads living into modern times in the Sahara. The Tuareg are a **Muslim** people.

ulama A **Muslim** religious expert or a scholar in Islamic law.

Additional Resources

Books

Ancient West African Kingdoms: Ghana, Mali, and Songhai
by Mary Quigley (Heinemann Library, 2002)

Empires of Medieval West Africa: Ghana, Mali, and Songhay
by David C. Conrad (Facts on File, 2005)

History and Activities of the West African Kingdoms
by Gary Barr (Heinemann Library, 2007)

West African Kingdoms
by John Haywood (Raintree, 2008)

West African Kingdoms: Empires of Gold and Trade
by Katherine E. Reece (Rourke Publishing, 2006)

Web Sites

http://africa.si.edu/exhibits/resources/mali/index.htm

http://web.cocc.edu/cagatucci/classes/hum211/CoursePack/coursepackpast/maligriot.htm

http://www.bbc.co.uk/worldservice/africa/features/storyofafrica/4chapter3.shtml

http://www.fordham.edu/halsall/source/1354-ibnbattuta.html

http://www.metmuseum.org/toah/hd/tsis/hd_tsis.htm

http://www.princetonol.com/groups/iad/lessons/middle/artmali.htm

http://www.ruf.rice.edu/~anth/arch/mali-interactive/index.html

http://www.wsu.edu:8080/~dee/CIVAFRCA/MALI.HTM

http://www.wsu.edu:8080/~wldciv/world_civ_reader/world_civ_reader_2/leo_africanus.html

INDEX

Acknowledgments

Alamy: 18 (Ariadne Van Zandbergen), 34 (John Warburton-Lee Photography); **The Art Archive:** 21 (John Webb), 24 (Ethnic Jewellery Exhibition Milan/Alfredo Dagli Orti), 37 (Private Collection/Marc Charmet), 49 (Antenna Gallery Dakar Senegal/Gianni Dagli Orti), 54 (Musée des Arts Africains et Océaniens/Alfredo Dagli Orti); **Bridgeman Art Library:** 1 (The Trustees of the Chester Beatty Library, Dublin), 13 (Heini Schneebeli), 25 (McBride, Angus), 32 (Heini Schneebeli), 36 (Michael Graham-Stewart), 40 (Horniman Museum, London, UK/Heini Schneebeli), 42 (The Trustees of the Chester Beatty Library, Dublin); **Corbis:** 4 (Gavin Hellier/JAI/), 5 (Nic Bothma/epa), 7 (Margaret Courtney-Clarke), 11 (Yann Arthus-Bertrand), 12 (Charles & Josette Lenars), 14 (Charles & Josette Lenars), 16 (Michael S. Lewis), 17 (Atlantide Phototravel), 19 (Remi Benali), 23 (Ralf-Finn Hestoft), 28 (Nik Wheeler), 29 (Christophe Boisvieux), 35 (Lindsay Hebberd), 38 (Charles & Josette Lenars), 39 (Remi Benali), 43 (Remi Benali), 44 (Nik Wheeler), 45 (Sandro Vannini), 48 (Olivier Martel), 50 (Charles & Josette Lenars), 52 (Sandro Vannini), 53 (Sebastien Cailleux), 58 (Atlantide Phototravel), 59 (Nic Bothma/epa); **iStockphoto.com:** 30 (Roberta Bianchi), 51 (Roberta Bianchi), 55 (Alan Tobey); **James Morris:** 20; **Werner Forman Archive:** 9, 22, 26 (Courtesy Entwistle Gallery), 27 (Courtesy Entwistle Gallery), 31, 33, 41, 46, 47 (Royal Museum of Central African Art, Tervuren), 56, 57.

Cover image: **The Art Archive** (John Webb)
Back cover image: **Shutterstock** (Joop Snijder, Jr.)

10/09